S.H.E Did It!

One Woman's Journey to Becoming Shameless, Healed, and Empowered.

The 3 P's of Life

Passion

Purpose

Perseverance

Sparkling Bwtee

S.H.E Did It!

One Woman's Journey to Becoming Shameless, Healed, and Empowered.

Tiffina Williams

Printed in the United States of America

First Printing, 2019

ISBN13: 9781947656987

The Butterfly Typeface Publishing
PO Box 56193
Little Rock AR 72215

Dedication

To my beautiful, sweet, and loving daughter, Triniti Una Williams. You have been the greatest inspiration, motivation, and encouragement in my life.

Because of YOU, a better mother and friend has been birthed in me. I am forever grateful for every lesson you've taught me. I love you with every fiber in my body, and nothing will change that!

I'm truly blessed and honored to be your mother.

I love you *Pretty, Pretty Cool Cat*!

Mommy

"She is worth far more than rubies..."
Proverbs 31:10

Table of Contents

"You Can and You Will"
Sparkling Bwtee

Foreword

History had it all wrong, it's economically more significant to cultivate strong women who thrive, surpass expectations and succeed. Women are the most important assets, to the circle of life, yet history has proven that societally, they have worse odds of upward mobility, than men.

Are you familiar with Victoria Woodhull, first female presidential candidate in 1872 and Shirley Chisholm, the first African American female presidential candidate in 1972? Those stories weren't discussed in school, but from an early age it's crucial to know that regardless of age, color, national origin, citizenship status, physical or mental disability, race, religion, creed, gender, sex, sexual orientation, gender identity and/or expression etc. you get to decide what you need to be. Victoria challenged the system 50 years prior to legally voting and Shirly, the same year the Equal Right Amendment was ratified. The broke the societal mode and surpassed expectations.

After reading stories about women's empowerment throughout history, I'm honored to offer a small piece to this book. What I love most about Tiffina, outside of being my favorite sibling, is that she will always hold everything to a high standard. Which is why I was taken aback, as a brother, husband, uncle and friend, to learn that I, too, play a part in the lives of so many women.

This book lets me know that it's important to be a good man, but it also reminds me that it's essential, to continuously uplift, respect and advocate for the women in my life and for all women.

I recently read a quote that resonated with me about reshaping perceptions and this book makes a strong argument for cultural inclusivity. It's important to understand why advocating growth and transformation internally, is key to changing external perceptions and alleviating boundaries. It gives you the tools to challenge your environment for positive affirmations, by starting at the core.

"We need to reshape our own perception of how we view ourselves. We have to step up as women and take the lead."
—Beyoncé

The one thing I realized after reading this book, is that this book was written for both women and men alike. It solidifies the importance of understanding our ability to rewrite our journey and not settle for mediocrity and our defining pasts. It delivers the truth behind lifting one another up and allowing the space for each of us to enhance our journey and ultimately decide what defines us.

Joseph Willis
Los Angeles 2019

Sparkling Love Notes

First and Foremost, I would like to thank GOD my Heavenly Father for this opportunity to tell my story for His glory. GOD has made all of this possible, and I'm forever grateful for His love towards me.

Secondly, I would like to thank my Main Man, my First Love, my Rock, my Dad, James Willis for always pushing me to do better, for pushing me to stay focused, for always correcting me from a place of love and wisdom, and for always coming to my rescue. You always told me as a child to "Look to learn and learn to look." I knew what you meant, and NOW, my dreams and purpose have made me learn to look.

My love for you will always and forever come from a True Daddy's girl heart.

Love always, Rudolph.

I would like to thank my Friend, my Helper, my PMW, and most importantly my Mom, Pamela Willis. My goal in life is to always make you happy and proud. I told you one day, "I was going to make you very proud of me (a different kind of proud). Well, today is the day!" I can't tell you enough how much I truly love you for just being there and for supporting me with everything. I will forever be your baby girl and your BEST friend.

I would like to thank my Protector Johnathan Willis and Baby Bear (my BFF), Joseph Willis. I've always wanted to make you both PROUD to say that you have a sister who is awesome. I love the stories that we share and how we laugh for hours when reminiscing on the good times. You all LOVE me, take care of me, and provide advice when necessary. I'm forever grateful for that. The joys, phone calls, smiles, and tears we share are the most important things to me. One thing our parents taught us was to "Take care of each other, we're all we have." And I will do this with every fiber in my body. When one of us makes it...WE ALL WIN! I love you both forever.

Thirdly, I would like to extend my appreciation to everyone including my special loves: the Waddells, the Willis, the Montgomerys, Latrice, Sunshine, the Lesters, my friends, aunts and uncles. You have inspired my life in ways I can't explain. You each played a special part in making me the woman I've become. I thank you for the respect, sowing of seeds, late night phone calls, love, words of wisdom, the prophecy from GOD, and the tears I've shared with you. I appreciate you all for believing in me and for pushing me into my purpose and passion. There would be no me, if there were no you, and I truly love you with a sincere and pure heart. My sparkle is brighter because of you!

Most importantly, thank you to all the women whose lives I've changed with my story. It's because of you that I needed to be strong and determined to become better. I thank you for allowing me to be transparent and truthful with you.

☆ Introduction

My Life "The Beginning"

"In the beginning God created..."
(Genesis 1:1)

"My Confidence is Authentic"
Sparkling Bwtee

My life began on December 7th, 1983. I was born and raised in St. Louis, Missouri to two loving parents, James and Pamela Willis. Together, they raised three beautiful children: two boys, Johnathan (the protector), Joseph (the baby bear), and the lovely middle child (and only daughter), me.

I weighed in at 5 lbs. 13 oz, and my parents were happy. But their world was immediately shaken up when the doctors told them that I wouldn't survive because I was so small. My parents didn't know what to do. They called my grandmother, Annie Ruth Willis, a sweet, Southern, hardworking, and a loving woman. They explained to her what the doctors had just told them.

"It's nothing wrong with her," Annie Ruth said with confidence, "She just hungry. Give her some cod liver oil with her milk and watch how quickly she fattens up!"

Now, if you know anything about a Southern grandmother and her touch, everything she does and says is always done out of love and wisdom.

Grandmother Annie had watched her mother and grandmother oversee many miracles, so she knew it would work.

My parents, though skeptical, took my grandmother's advice, and long story short, I'm alive. And to this day, food is my best friend!

I'm the happiest where food is involved, especially if it's something sweet or ice cream!

I survived!

A True and Funny Story

My parents had me in 1983 and exactly two years later, my brother, Joseph, was born.

That day, my mother was planning my 2nd birthday party. Her sister (my aunt) kept asking if my mother wanted her to take me to the celebration.

My mother said, "No," and they kept arguing back and forth.

After a while, my mother began having contractions, and my little brother became my birthday present.

Growing up, Joseph and I always had birthday parties together. We shared one cake; his side was a boy cake, and my side was more often than not, a princess cake. This was normal for us, until we were old enough to want our own cakes, to want separate birthday parties, and to have friends over.

My parents gave in to this idea, and it changed my life forever.

I've always said that Joseph was my twin. If he got hurt, I could feel it on the opposite side of my body. If he was sad, I could feel it, and I would call him or go check on him. This is a bond that can never be broken.

I love you, Baby Bear!

As a teenager in high school, it really challenged me to be different.

My older brother, Johnathan, was a grade ahead of me. He was my protector.

Boys would try to date me or talk to me, but Johnathan would interfere.

"Dude," Johnathan would shout. "You are NOT dating my sister!"

When the boys told me Johnathan was doing this, I was sad. Some of those guys were cute!

Whether I liked it or not, Johnathan was always around for everything. He made sure I got to class safely. I loved how protective he was. It made me feel good inside. I knew he cared about me.

I love you, Johnathan; thank you for always protecting me, by any means necessary!

My parents were strict and protective of me as well. I couldn't go over to people's houses, spend the night, or even hang out with random individuals.

I HATED THAT!

I felt like I missed out on so many things while I was in school.

I didn't get to go on my senior class trip to Cancun, Mexico because there wasn't an adult chaperone.

I couldn't wear shorts above my knees and wearing anything tight was out of the question.

I couldn't hang out after school unless it was for a valid reason, usually a school educational program or an assembly but definitely nothing fun!

And for prom, I had to have my oldest brother drive me to the school in our burgundy Astro Van! My dad picked me up afterward.

They did allow me to go to the hotel party after the prom, and that was fun.

Freedom didn't come until I graduated from Affton High School in 2002 when I went straight to college.

I didn't know what I wanted to major in so I just concentrated on general studies, hoping that something would catch my interest.

College wasn't really what I wanted to do, but my parents convinced me to try it for a year, and I did.

However, there was a part of me that felt I wasn't mentally ready for college. I wanted some chill time.

However, I went anyway and began taking out loans to pay for school. Once I saw how much my financial aid refund checks were every semester, I began to just go for the checks.

I passed some of the classes, and after the year was up, I stopped going.

I was working at Walgreens at the same time, and my money was looking good. I started partying with my friends, and soon, I decided to get my own place. I also tried to get my driver's license.

I'm doing good, I thought to myself.

I liked nice things, and looking cute was a priority, so I knew I had to work. As soon as I got money, I blew it on clothes, shoes, jewelry, and getting my nails and hair done.

I didn't have any real bills, just my cellphone. Saving wasn't important to me. Looking cute was.

My parents kept saying, "Save for a rainy day. You never know when you will need it."

"For even when we were with you,
this we commanded you, that if any would not work,
neither should he eat."
(2 Thessalonians 3:10)

I didn't listen.

Three years later, I got fired, but I found another job quickly.

I knew that, in order to have the life I wanted, I had to work. So, I worked hard. I was focused and determined that nothing would keep me from having the life I wanted.

While living under my parents' roof, my life began to change.

So did my desires.

Shameless | Healed | Empowered

"New Day, New Horizons, New Levels"
Sparkling Bwtee

_____

_____

_____

_____

_____

_____

_____

_____

_____

_____

_____

_____

_____

_____

_____

"Self-Love is the best Love."
Sparkling Bwtee

☆ Chapter One

When the Breaking Happens

"When I was a child, I spake as a child, I understood as a child, I thought as a child: but when I became a man (Woman), I put away childish things."
1 Corinthians 13:11

"Cheering for All Women to Win."
Sparkling Bwtee

I was seventeen, a high school graduate, a freshman in college, a virgin, and eager to see what the world had to offer.

Up to that point, my life was pretty structured. It consisted of work, college, church, church, and more church.

I learned how to catch the bus to places I needed to go. I got credit cards, and now, more than ever, I was free and focused on my teenage lifestyle which meant I was interested in keeping up with the fads.

The girls my age were partying and wearing tight clothes. I no longer wanted to be on the outside looking in. I wanted to be a part of this exciting life.

I was ready. At least, I thought I was.

I started wearing clothes that I liked, versus what my parents wanted me to wear.

Tight clothes became a thing for me, and I was loving it!

Part of my dad's responsibility at the church was opening and closing the church. Thus forth, we had to be there all the time: Tuesday night Bible study, Wednesday night choir rehearsal, Friday night revival, Sunday morning church, and Evening service too.

I was getting tired of going to church every time the doors opened, and since I didn't have a car at the time, I couldn't do much in the evenings.

I was going to church because I had to, not because I was interested in developing a relationship with God.

I knew who He was, but the relationship hadn't developed yet.

One night at church, there was a guy there. I noticed him watching me, and I was watching him too. We did a little flirting, but it wasn't a big deal.

We had kind of grown up in the church, and our families knew each other very well. We were cool.

He and I laughed and talked the entire time. That was that.

At another church service, there he was again.

I was looking super cute that day. I was wearing a long denim skirt, a white fitted t-shirt I had tucked inside my skirt, and some sandals.

Baby, I was the cutest one there! You couldn't tell me anything that day!

He and I laughed and talked.

"You should call me some time," he said.

"Sure," I said. "Give me your number."

He wrote his number and pager number on a green post it and slid it to me. I gave him mine as well.

I was so HAPPY!

I stuck the number inside of a journal that I carried with me everywhere. I put the journal in my purse.

When I got home that night, I pulled it out and looked at it several times before going to bed.

I was smiling wildly from the excitement!

After waiting a few days (I didn't want to seem too eager), I paged him, and he called me right back.

I picked up right away and was on cloud nine. Talking to him was fun, relaxing, and easy. He seemed like a cool, laid-back kind of dude.

Our conversations were long, funny, and meaningful. We shared what we wanted out of life, where we hoped to go, and what we expected from each other.

This was on track to being something serious!

A few months later, I turned eighteen. We had our first real date on my actual birthday.

He picked me up in his Chevy Silverado and even brought flowers!

How sweet was that?

We ate at Applebee's and ordered from the 2 for $20 menu. We laughed, talked, and enjoyed the night.

The more I got to know him and hang out with him, the more comfortable I became around him.

Soon, we were hanging out all the time, enjoying movies, dinner, and spending time with his friends and family. We also enjoyed chill nights of watching Blockbuster movies at home.

I mean I was all up in it!

It felt good to have his undivided attention. He seemed real and genuine.

Staying out late, partying, drinking, and premarital sex were also things we did. I was willing to do anything to impress him.

Being with him was fun. It wasn't long before I was ALL in!

Even though he was a sweet guy and just what I *thought* I wanted, the warning signals were loud. Nevertheless, I didn't want to hear or accept them because the relationship was what I wanted.

People were telling me not to mess with him because he 'wasn't right,' was a 'player,' and he 'used girls.'

No matter how much they told me that he wasn't right for me and that he didn't treat women well, I refused to listen.

I'm different, I thought. *He won't do me like that.*

I wanted him, and I spoke up for him in the most mature and confident manner I could muster. Besides, I wanted to see for myself.

It wasn't long before I began to see the red flags for myself.

Soon, I began to see things that I hadn't seen before. His calls to me became less frequent, and there were times when he wouldn't even return my calls.

He began to hang out late at night and would not return home until the sun came up the next morning.

What's up with this, I thought.

I didn't see what was coming.

We began to argue.

"Hey," I said with hurt and concern. "You didn't call me back, and I called you like six times, but no answer."

He always had an excuse.

"I didn't hear the phone," he'd say with an attitude, or, "I was with my family."

When he noticed that I was paying attention to his behavior, he seemed to care even less about what he was doing. He knew that I believed his excuses, even though they were made up at best.

The lies became more prevalent, and he even began cheating.

By this time, we'd been dating for almost a year.

The mysterious phone calls and text messages were just the beginning of the breakdown in our relationship.

He began to verbally and mentally abuse me as well. He'd lie about his whereabouts and would go MIA whenever he felt like it.

I began to push back and would fuss, cuss, and argue with him. I just couldn't understand how this sweet guy could hurt me this way.

Through all this (even staying up late waiting by the phone to see if he would call me), I never missed work, and I would call him all day to check on him. Then, I'd get an attitude because he was out doing God knows what.

We argued day in and day out. I'd get an attitude and stop talking. Then, I'd withhold sex from him. I just didn't want to be bothered with him.

I was pissed!

He knew I was mad and would buy me things to make up and swindle me back into his good graces.

At this time, it didn't matter, and I didn't care how he treated me. I was in love and blinded by my feelings towards him, so much so, that he didn't have to prove he meant it.

There were times I would get dressed up and wait for him to show up, only to have him not show up at all.

I was a broken woman inside. I wanted him to notice my outer appearance because he clearly did not notice me.

So, I tried everything I could think of to get his attention, and nothing did.

We broke up for a few weeks. He called and begged for me to come back, and eventually, I would go back.

That became a pattern repeated more times than I can recall. We'd break up, make up, break up, and make up, only to break up again.

This cycle was on repeat and kept skipping.

Things went from bad to worse when I found out I was pregnant. I was scared out of my mind.

How could I let my parents down? I couldn't let them or anyone else find out. I was still living under their roof, unmarried and unprepared for a baby!

I was afraid and didn't know what to do!

Ever since I was a kid, I'd heard in church how important it was to be married and not have a baby out of wedlock. I also knew how important it was for me to wait until I was not only physically mature, but mentally mature to have a baby. I knew my mind was not ready.

Finally, I gained enough courage to confide in someone I trusted, and she gave me some advice.

"You can't mess up your life right now," she said matter-of-factly. "You're too young for this."

She told me where I could go to get an abortion, and she said that no one would know. She wrote down the information and said, "Call them to schedule an appointment in the morning."

I fought with the decision long and hard. I went back and forth. I knew what had been taught to me in my home and at church about abortions. Convictions and worry set in. I didn't want to disappoint my parents, and I knew it was dead wrong.

How could I even consider such an option?

I felt like my only options were to tell my parents and hurt and embarrass them or to do what I thought was right for me.

There were many sleepless nights while I weighed those options. I tossed and turned but finally chose to have an abortion.

I couldn't believe I had found myself in that situation.

To my surprise, he went with me to the appointment, stayed with me afterwards, and took care of me.

"Are you sure about this?" He asked.

I nodded my head yes, but *how can you be ok with such a choice?*

After the procedure, he took me home and didn't leave my side. He catered to me; it made me feel special and loved again. I knew he would change and go back to the old him.

I had hoped for this.

A few days later, I was back to normal physically and saw a different side of him.

He was the sweet, loving, and kind guy I fell for in the beginning.

I was different too.

Although I had sat with the decision to terminate my pregnancy, I wasn't settled with the choice. I had nightmares, crying spells, fear, and frustration.

Had I really just killed my baby?

I felt so alone. I didn't have anyone I could talk to about what I'd done. No one knew how I was feeling.

So, I buried my feelings.

Since I couldn't talk to him, I dealt with the pain in my own way.

I began to shut down.

The more time went on, the more hurt I felt. I hurt like never before.

The questions were endless.

Why did I do it? Why didn't I just say no? Why? Why? Why?

I couldn't answer any of those questions. I convinced myself that God hated me for the decision I made.

I was lost!

I prayed and asked God to forgive me for this mistake and promised I wouldn't do it again.

Then, I pulled myself together as best I could, got up, and went back to work.

However, I found myself staring off into space while thinking about the abortion. I'd see babies and burst into tears.

I couldn't explain it.

I became quiet and tried to detach myself from him.

I didn't call or text him for a few days. I was dealing with the hurt all by myself.

I felt stuck and didn't know what to do.

I became isolated, lonely, and afraid. I felt unloved.

All I ever wanted from him was for him to love me, to be honest, and to give me his attention.

He apologized for his actions and said things would be better. But nothing eased the pain.

I forgave him, but unfortunately, the cycle of abuse continued. He never did change; by this time we were living together under one roof. The foundation of our relationship was still not solid. It was broken.

Another abortion, *What? How? Not again*, and another one after that. The last two were the hardest for me because I had no support from him. He didn't show me any love or comfort. I was left alone to handle all three by myself. It was rough.

I begged God to forgive me and vowed that I wouldn't do it again.

"I had to understand where I was in order to know where I was going."
Sparkling Bwtee

"Address your PAIN; it's NOT okay to keep suffering."
Sparkling Bwtee

"My Confidence is Authentic."
Sparkling Bwtee

☆ Chapter Two

When the Breaking Happens

"The words of the reckless pierce like swords,
but the tongue of the wise brings healing."
Proverbs 12:18

"More God, More Sparkle!"
Sparkling Bwtee

By now, I was sure God hated me and didn't love me anymore. I was sure I was going to Hell.

I was alone.

To make matters worse, his verbal abuse got worse. He said things like:

"You're so dumb. You're stupid. You don't matter. You make a person want to cheat. You're a retard. You're not good enough. I can't stand you. You're a dumbass. You don't do anything to keep a man happy. You're ugly."

His words not only hurt me, they destroyed me. I was slowly losing myself.

I felt useless, unworthy, and undeserving of anything better. He continued making promises that he was going to change and that he was sorry for what he had done. Still, I continued to stay.

I was hoping he would love me the right way. When he said he was sorry, it felt genuine. When he promised that his behavior would change, I believed him.

Nonetheless, he didn't care enough about me, and I didn't care enough about me either. All I wanted was him – EVERYTHING about him.

Again, I tried to impress him and to keep him interested. I began trying to buy his love. I maxed out my credit cards, used up my savings account, bought clothes and shoes for him, paid for dinners, and paid his tickets and court fines.

You name it. I did it, just to keep him happy.

I felt that I needed his apologies in order to heal wounds that his words created.

He would promise that he loved me and that he would stop. I'd take him back time and time again.

I felt like I needed him to make me complete. I knew my love for him was real, but I couldn't get him to show me that his love for me was real.

Since loving him was the only romantic love I'd know, I began to rationalize it and thought this was how I was supposed to be treated.

I was young and uninformed.

I continued to believe that he was what I wanted.

He knew all the right things to say.

"I want to marry you," He'd promise. "You're the only one for me."

But nothing happened.

Pressure from his family came too.

"You need to marry this girl," his family said. "She's pretty, smart, got her head on straight, and she's a good church girl."

But nothing happened.

Then, we began looking at rings.

But nothing happened.

People were also asking questions.

"When are you going to have a baby," they'd ask. "You all have been together so long. You might as well make him a dad."

Those questions hurt and threatened to send me back into a depression.

I held it together and said, "If I don't have kids by the time I turn 28, I'm not having any."

That bought me a little time and peace. They left me alone about having babies.

Besides, I wanted to be a wife before I had kids. I knew I loved him enough to change him back into the sweet man that he was in the beginning, if only he'd married me.

Everything still continued, and nothing changed. I began to accept his behavior as normal.

My house, faith, finances, and relationship were in shambles.

I was a broken and damaged woman on the inside, but I was careful not to reveal it on the outside.

I covered up and disguised my pain very well. I wanted others to think that everything was all good.

But the writing was on the wall for the world to see. When you're broken on the inside, it will bleed out no matter how much you try to cover it up with your outer appearance.

> *"For nothing is secret, that shall not be made manifest; neither anything hid, that shall not be known and come abroad." (Luke 8:17)*

All while pulling away and trying to cover up how I felt on the inside, it started making me think about a few things. I began reaching out to family and friends for help. I also told them about the problems.

I spilled the beans!

They had advice.

"You should leave. Get out. Quit allowing him to do that to you. That's not real love. I can't believe he would do that."

My judgment was so clouded. I didn't know what to do.

I started questioning myself again.

Why is he doing this to me? Why doesn't he love me like he says he does? Am I what he wants?

We talked about all of these questions, and he assured me that he did love me, that things would definitely change, and that I was the only one he wanted.

Years later, in 2010, I married him despite all the arguing, holding out on sex, cheating, lies, me pulling away, warnings from others about what type of guy he was, verbal abuse, and going MIA from time to time because I knew that once we were married, all of that would stop.

He said he would change, and I believed him. "I'm tired of my behavior," he'd insist. "I will stop doing this to you. I love you too much to keep hurting you this way." And I believed him.

I believed that a wedding ceremony was the change we needed.

Now that I was his wife, he would finally respect me.

Well, the verbal and mental abuse continued.

I had been looking for love in all the wrong places and from someone who was unwilling or incapable of giving it to me.

I needed something to make me feel complete.

I was working, and I decided to go back to school. Although I was still partying, I did go to church from time to time. But nothing seemed to satisfy or complete me the way I wanted.

December rolled around, and it was my birthday weekend. I had plans to go to a club and was determined to have a good time.

I got dressed and was looking good! I was ready to celebrate! All my friends showed up and I was excited.

At the club, there was smoking, drinks being passed around, shots being taken, and plenty of dancing.

Then, I began to get hot and felt weak.

I ordered a cranberry juice to see if that would help.

"I need to go to the bathroom," I told one of my friends.

I walked quickly because I felt sick. I instantly started vomiting once I got there.

What's up with this, I wondered.

Well, remember when I said I began telling people that I wasn't going to have children if I didn't have any by the time I was 28?

Happy 28th birthday to me! I was pregnant.

It was only a year into our marriage, and this time, I was determined to keep the baby, no matter what.

I had spoken it, the best way I knew how, and I know God allowed it to happen for me.

Just when I thought things were turning around for me, the enemy came right in and tried to steal, to kill, and to destroy me yet again.

> *The thief comes only to steal and kill and destroy;*
> *(John 10:10)*

Six weeks into my pregnancy, I found out that my husband had cheated on me with another woman.

I was devastated, and I thought, *How could he do this to me? Why did I continue with this guy? We're married now, and he did this to me?*

I hated his behavior and the sight of him disgusted me. I didn't want him anymore, but I didn't know how to get out.

"It's Time to Act, Change and Trust"
Sparkling Bwtee

_____

_____

_____

_____

_____

_____

_____

_____

"Faith In, Fear Out!"
Sparkling Bwtee

☆ **Chapter Three**

"The Mending of My Broken Pieces"

---

*"God, pick up the pieces. Put me back together again.
You are my praise!"*
Jeremiah 17:4

"My Reveal is About to Bless You!"
Sparkling Bwtee

One of the hardest decisions to make is deciding if you should stay or walk away from all the things that you've ever known.

I prayed and asked God to fix my situation. I wanted out. The only problem with it was I didn't trust that God would do it. I was afraid that He didn't love me enough, since I had done what I had done.

My lack of faith had me untrusting, afraid and worried. I beat myself up so many times. Although I tried with everything in me, I couldn't fix it on my own.

"And he saith unto them, why are ye fearful, O ye of little faith? Then he arose and rebuked the winds and the sea; and there was a great calm." (Matthew 8:26)

I desperately needed God to fix my situation. I was rushing Him to fix something that I hadn't completely given over to Him. This was clear since I had left my husband, but I kept going back. I wasn't strong enough to let it go.

The LOVE was there for the guy, but I desperately wanted this nightmare to end. When I settled for a counterfeit type of love, anything that he did became what I accepted.

Why? Because I wanted it to be real.

The pregnancy was easy, but the pain that I was dealing with from him was hard. The Lies, my emotions, fights, no money, almost homeless, arguments, cheating verbal abuse, the make ups, break ups, and cussing all continued. I hoped this baby was going to be a blessing for me, I needed a chance to have someone love me and it be real.

Thank God for my daughter. She was the answer to my prayers; she gave me an out. Having her allowed me to shift my focus. I started paying more attention to her, loving her, teaching her, and whatever else she needed.

On top of working full-time, I went to the gym, shopped, or did *anything* to avoid facing going home and facing my problem. But I wanted my little family to work.

In my mind, I had invested too much time in the relationship to let it all go to waste. I wasn't about to give up.

As I said before, I was looking for someone to complete me. All of those things made me feel complete and whole!

I asked myself a serious question, "If you need those things to complete you, where is there room for God to do the mending, the breaking, and the removing that you're asking Him for?"

I got tired of worrying, being broke, busted, disgusted, feeling less than, not enough, unwanted, undesired, upset, and frustrated.

I started going back to church and I began to pray.

Lord,

I know that I don't have a real relationship with you, I pray sometimes and believe other times. I know that You can hear me. Forgive me for my past mistakes. I come before Your throne of grace asking You to help in these areas that I am afraid to let out and to let go of. I am coming before You because You know my broken areas.

I need You to step in and to release this hold that these things have on me. I'm not perfect, and I know that I have made mistakes in the past, but I know You to be a healer, deliver, and a provider for me. Lord, please don't let me go until You see that I am ready for this growth to take place. You said in Your Word to Ask and it shall be given unto you. Seek and ye shall find. Knock and the door shall be opened. I'm asking, knocking, and seeking You, God. I SHALL not give up until You bless me out of this mess. I'm prepared for what You have for me to handle next. Prepare me for the separation of those things...and help me become ready for My NEXT Level! It will NOT look like the last level I was just in.

In Jesus Name,

Amen.

One thing I knew I wasn't going to do was give up on God. I had a church relationship with God, but not a personal relationship with Him.

I was ashamed, hurt, prideful, broken, bitter, and afraid to let God take control.

So, I kept on doing what I wanted and prayed for His grace and mercy daily.

When I tell you that God is a keeper, He kept me even in my mess. He kept blessing me. I NEVER went without anything. Even though I didn't make much money, I was able to pay my bills, to buy food, and to pay my daughter's tuition for school. NOTHING was ever cut off, late, or behind, and in the midst of all of this, I was caring for my child too.

God said in His Word that He is a rewarder to those who diligently seek Him.

> *"... for he that cometh to God must believe that he is, and that he is a rewarder of them that diligently seek him."*
> *(Hebrews 11:6)*

So, I decided to do just that. I began to seek the Lord because I was tired, and I didn't know any other way out. I was over the mental abuse, verbal abuse, lack of love, being cheated on, disrespected as his wife, and being used up.

God hears you, sees you, knows you, and will come see about you when you use your 'sound.'

My 'sound' was what He needed to hear so that He could respond with,

"Daughter, I'm coming to rescue you from this."

When God heard my sound, He came running, but I had to prepare myself to let go and to let Him do it.

I was ready! I started writing plans, goals, and dreams of what life looked like with me being happy. I wasn't completely healed, yet I was in the process of my healing.

I began posting on social media to encourage, to uplift and to empower women.

I wrote to free myself in hopes that other women would be able to see just how God was transitioning me from *adaptability* to *accessibility*.

God needed me more!

"My Shame and Stains won't remain."
Sparkling Bwtee

_____

_____

_____

_____

_____

_____

_____

_____

"Shameless and Still Cute!"
Sparkling Bwtee

☆ Chapter Four

"The Healing Process"

"He will wipe every tear from their eyes. There will be no more death' or mourning or crying or pain, for the old order of things has passed away."
Revelations 21:4

"Forgiveness is the BEST part of my journey."
Sparkling Bwtee

With tears flowing down my face, I repented and asked God for forgiveness and cried out to Him. I needed His deliverance and help like never before.

I was tired of being tired.

In order to encourage myself and to lift my spirit, I began writing, reading my Bible, and listening to motivational speakers.

Several different people suggested that I write my story.

"If the Lord sees fit," I responded, "He will do it."

In 2015, God dropped it in my spirit to start a blog.

"Huh," I said with much confusion. "Lord, what am I going to write about?"

"Your story," God spoke back to me.

"What about my story," I asked, still apprehensive.

He spoke again, "I'm bringing you out so you can help other women come out. Your story needs to be heard."

To that I replied, "Okay, God. I hear You."

I didn't have a name for the blog nor a site. So, I went back to God.

Specifically, I asked, "God, what shall I name it?" I wanted something that would represent me and who I was becoming.

He immediately began to download everything I needed: the name, the website address, and the content. God gave me the name Sparkling Bwtee (Beauty).

I was excited! The name was amazing for me.

I went back to God and asked Him what did B W T E E stand for. Three days later, He said, "Beautiful Women Together Encouraging Each Other."

I replied, "God, that is amazing!"

I had to get still enough not only for Him to speak, but for me to listen. I was happy and overjoyed that this was actually happening for me. I began thanking God for this opportunity.

I started writing, and four years later, the blog is now part of my ministry. I wrote about things that I'd been through in my marriage, motherhood, life, and anything that would encourage, motivate, inspire or uplift other women.

Writing helped ease the pain I was going through, but I was very much still in it.

I got all the way back in church; no more ins and outs. I wanted and longed for a real relationship with God. I knew Him and I wanted to experience Him.

I went through separation after separation only to get back together. It was rough.

The last time we separated was different. Somehow, I knew it would be the final time. I had gained confidence in myself, and I knew what God could do on my behalf.

God knew that I was ready this time. I was tired, and I surrendered it all to Him. Finally, when I was strong enough, the break happened.

Another True Story

It was the day before our six-year wedding anniversary. We were arguing and had not been on good terms that day. But later that evening, we got dressed up and attended a Chaka Khan concert.

I mean we had tickets already and good seats at the Fox Theater, so why not, right?

I was rocking, jamming, and having a good old time while looking beautiful. I had fun.

Once the concert ended, we rode home in silence, got home, and went to bed.

Before, I got in bed, I whispered to God, "If You get me out of this situation, I promise I won't go back."

I tossed and turned all night long. I was in and out of sleep. Finally, God spoke loud and clear to me. He said, "Now, it's time!"

Shaking and trembling, I got out of bed, walked into the living room, and said a quick prayer:

"God, I will NOT go back again. I'm done, and please give me the strength and confidence to know that I can do this without him."

In Jesus' name,

Amen.

God spoke again. "I will take care of you."

That was the confidence I needed. It happened just that quick!

I walked back into the bedroom, and he was laying there on his phone.

"I think," I began calmly, "that it's time for you to go."

"What," he said now irritated.

So, I said it again. "Yes," this time with more certainty in my voice. "It is time for you to go. I can't do this anymore!"

He started getting loud, cussed, and fussed while he gathered his things. But this time, I was unbothered by any of it because I was finally getting the peace that I'd wanted and now knew that I deserved.

God knew that this time when I asked Him to help me, I was ready for something to change. He knew that this was my last plea, and He knew that I was ready to step out of my false sense of comfort and control and that I was ready to allow Him to get me out.

God did not turn His back on me. He loved me that much. He saw where I was headed, and He didn't want me to continue to become shipwrecked with all that was going on in my life.

God will save you out of your mess before your mess turns into a worse situation.

The mothers from the church would always say, "Hey may not come when you want Him to, but He will be there right on time."

God came and pulled me right up out of my mess, and I NEVER looked back! I got out and stayed out.

I shifted my focus to what God had for me to do, and my work has just begun.

This ended in a divorce, and I can now say, "I am FREE, shameless, healed, and empowered!"

Things began to turn around in my favor, and I was truly living my life.

I was happy and content. Life was so much better now that God had brought me out of the dark place.

The God I serve knew that I was in a comfortable place of discontent. He knew that things needed to be shaken up to test my faith.

"And Jesus said unto them, because of your unbelief; for verily I say unto you if ye have faith as a grain of a mustard seed, you shall say unto this mountain, move hence to yonder place; and it shall be moved and nothing shall be impossible unto you." (Matthew 17:20)

I had the faith, I believed, and God delivered. But He wasn't done with me. He wanted me to have more than just a little bit. Now, He need more from me.

I had been renting a house for more than five years, and occasionally, I'd mention to God that I wanted to own my home. I wanted more space and the freedom to do whatever I wanted to do inside of it.

There was a death in our family, and I needed to travel for the funeral.

The landlord called and said, "We need to talk."

"Okay," I said right away wondering what was wrong. A million things ran through my mind.

He came over and said, "We like you staying here, but you will either have to pay more rent or move out."

I sat there through the rest of the meeting with him and made notes.

"What do you plan on doing?" He asked finally.

I had so much to consider: my daughter, work, my location, finances, school, travel, etc. I mean everything.

"Well," I said slowly. "I would have to think about it."

"I can give you a few days to make a decision," he said as he got up to leave.

I began to cry. I cried hard and began to talk to God.

"Lord, how could you do this to me," I sobbed. "What am I going to do about my daughter? This is horrible for them to do this to me!"

Immediately, I became convicted. With tears still flowing down my face, I began to speak these words, *"Lord, whatever this is, I trust you! "*

My faith was tested, but not defeated. The Lord was saying, "Do you trust Me, or do you trust what man has for you?

I went out of town, and when I returned, I called the landlord.

"I will move out," I said with bold confidence.

I had no idea where I was going or what to do next. However, I trusted that God would take care of me like He said He would.

My credit was good, so the next day, I contacted a realtor to help me with the process of looking for a new home.

We made an appointment. I sat down to talk about what steps to take. With each step I took, I prayed first.

The realtor asked me where I wanted to place my home loan and I decided I wanted it to be at the same bank as my car loan. I was hesitant because I was denied for another credit union, so fear kind of set in.

I did everything she and the mortgage company advised me to do and submitted an application to see if I qualified.

They ran a few numbers and did a credit check. To my surprise, after completing the necessary paperwork, I was approved within two days!

I was happy!

On the fourth day, I was sent my approval letter; I began looking for houses.

There were several houses I looked at and considered, but they were not the right fit.

God said to write the vision and to make it plain. In February of 2018, I had already drawn and written what kind of house I wanted.

In the meantime, things were happening.

I gave my realtor $500 in earnest money, and she deposited it before the time which caused my checking account to become overdrawn.

What in the world is happening? I thought.

I was mad, and I told God just how mad I was. Again, conviction set in, and in the midst of my trial, I still said, "God, I trust You."

> *"God will perfect everything that concerns you."*
> *(Psalm 138:8)*

I went on with everything as normal.

I called my mom, and she did what mothers do.

"What do you need to help cover?"

"Nothing," I replied confidently. "I'm perfectly fine. God will provide what I need."

I wasn't worried. I went on with my day as usual. Later, I checked the mail and discovered a check that was double what I needed to clear my overdrawn account!

Instantly, I began praising and worshipping God. I knew that it was all Him. I hadn't been worried. I trusted and believed that He would take care of me like He said. I was faithful over a few things, and He made me ruler over many.

"... You have been faithful with a few things; I will put you in charge of many things." (Matthew 25:23)

I trust God at His word. I went looking for it because it was my heart's desire. God said it. I knew and believed it was true.

My realtor was going out of town for a few days, and the day before she left, I said, "I want to go see this house before you leave. It is my house. This is it. This is the one." I repeated.

"I'm busy today," she said, "But I can have someone else take you out to see it."

"No," I said. "I will wait."

I kept looking and praying over the house all weekend, and on Tuesday when she came back, she called me.

"The house has had many views. A bidder had bid on it already."

I thought, "Lord, let the deal fall through because I want it."

"Let's go see these other houses on your list first," she said.

My mind was made up, but I agreed.

As we were driving, she quickly took a U-turn and went a different way.

"Mommy," my daughter said, "where is she going?"

"I don't know baby," I said just as shocked and confused as she was. "We will see."

As we drove, it became clear that we were driving to the house I had my heart set on.

I knew that whatever was going on was nothing but God's doing! Those other houses were not my heart's desire.

Hallelujah!

When we walked into the house, I felt at peace and right at home. I began to cry.

"God, this is what I want."

I'm here to tell you that in May 2018, I walked into my dream house with no money down and extra money in my escrow. I got money off the closing price of my NOW home.

One of my favorite scriptures to reflect on is this:

"And without faith it is impossible to please God, because anyone who comes to him must believe that he exists and that he rewards those who earnestly seek him." (Hebrews 11:6)

I seek God about everything that happens in life. Nothing's too big or too small for me to take to Him in prayer.

I'm faithful to His Word. I trust Him at His Word, and I wait on His Word to manifest in my life.

For that, I will forever praise God with everything I have.

When God pushes you out of your comfort zone, it means that He has something BETTER for you. God knew that the comfort zone I was in it would have killed me or kept me stagnant for too long. He needed me for more.

Thank You, Lord!

The tears wouldn't stop flowing.

God turned my mess into my victory! He
will do the same for you!

"Flawed and Still Worthy!"
Sparkling Bwtee

_____

_____

_____

_____

_____

_____

_____

_____

☆ Chapter Five

"The Victorious Run"

"But thanks be to God! He gives us the victory through our Lord Jesus Christ."
1 Corinthians 15:57

*"Undo the folds in your life
and create goals in your life."*
Sparkling Bwtee

During my victory run, I was able to forgive myself!

I can't change what I did or what happened. Nevertheless, I can change how I respond to it by letting GO and watching for the GLOW.

The GLOW is the light of Jesus that lives inside of me.

As I mentioned in a previous chapter, I was told that I should write a book.

"And the LORD answered me, and said, Write the vision, and make it plain upon tables, that he may run that readeth it." (Habakkuk 2:2)

After the blog, I began to write. Here we are now in 2019, and I've written my first book!

My journey may not make sense to you. Maybe, you will look at me differently.

You may even judge me because of my past. However, this journey was what God allowed me to experience so that I could show others (especially women) how strong they can be with God's help. They can overcome any obstacle thrown their way.

Learning how to make room for God in your life will cause things to happen that you won't be able to explain.

Making room for God is about being obedient when He tells you to do something and not second guessing what He's said or asked you to do.

Walk confidently, boldly, and courageously in whom He created you to be!

God knew that this is what I would do in my life.

He never stopped loving me regardless of all the mistakes I made. He never gave up on me. I got the victory!

This victory run has produced so many things for me. I can't even begin to explain.

"For I know the plans I have for you," declares the LORD, "plans to prosper you and not to harm you, plans to give you hope and a future." (Jeremiah 29:11)

Once I let go of the plans I made, plans that didn't line up with the will of God, my circumstances began to change for the better.

I became grounded in what God needed me to do, and I began the work. The work included: healing, separation, wisdom, understanding, guidance, teaching, and patience in the journey.

I had to protect what I was carrying to prevent everything back in that God had moved out.

God has rewritten my story for the better.

He has taken all the broken pieces in my life and used them for His glory.

Now, I am a 35-year-old survivor. I am also a happily divorced single mom. I am self-confident, worthy, and a deserving woman of God.

I'm also a homeowner. I have a good job working from home. Every bill is paid, and I have my own ministry that God has built specifically for me.

My ministry has blossomed into a T-shirt line that women can boldly and confidently wear. These shirts are a proclamation to all that no matter what has happened in your life, you can still come out better than you went it.

SHAME has to stop!

HEALING needs to take place.

EMPOWERING is best.

Stop allowing your past experiences to determine your worth. You are not what you've done. You are what God says you are!

You are the next #S.H.E Shameless... Healed... Empowered, Bw-Teeful Woman God created you to be!

God is a keeper when you want to be kept!

I now live exceedingly and abundantly with acceleration. God did it!

I know it's hard, but don't give up the fight.

Push until the end, and you will have a victorious run. Your testimony will be like mine, "Only God did it!"

"She opens her mouth with wisdom; and on her tongue is the law of kindness." (Proverbs 31:26)

You are a Proverbs 31 Woman!

All it took for me to change was getting out of God's way so He could do for me what He'd already planned.

God had **MORE** for me.

I am **MORE** happy than I've ever been.

I am **MORE** wise than I've ever been.

I am **MORE** sound in whom God created in me.

I'm living in the overflow of God's goodness and mercy.

Go out and sparkle with a purpose.

Be blessed!

"I don't need permission to be great, I was born great." **Sparkling Bwtee**

It's My Season. It's My Time.
It's My Now!
Sparkling Bwtee

_____

_____

_____

_____

_____

_____

_____

_____

_____

_____

_____

_____

_____

_____

_____

"You GLOW up girl!"
Sparkling Bwtee

☆ Conclusion

What I Want You to Know

Delight yourself in the LORD, and he will give you the desires of your heart.
Psalm 37:4

"Sparkle with a Purpose."
Sparkling Bwtee

When you hold on to things that no longer fit with who you are or what you represent, it's harder to break free from them.

Imagine a flower: the flower has roots that are in the ground. What things are needed for growth? Soil, water, and sunlight, right?

Being in a toxic relationship is like planting a flower in soil that has been poisoned. The flower can't thrive in this condition.

If you're in an environment that consists of hurtful words and actions, it is poison to you. Just like the flower that can't thrive in a toxic environment, you can't thrive either.

I was holding on to something that didn't benefit me.

Because I was in such a toxic environment, my thinking was negatively impacted. I thought I could change him. I thought that by marrying him, he would respect me since I would be his wife.

There is one thing I need you to know. You can't change a person. They can change if they want to, but the work is for them to do.

An unchanged person produces an unchanged environment. Sometimes, the only way to break the cycle is to leave.

I had asked him why so many times, and his response was always the same.

"I didn't do that. They are lying on me."

I had to realize that a solution can never be reached unless a person is willing to acknowledge the problem.

I was tired of it all. I wanted to break free from the situation, but I didn't know how.

I couldn't let go of him. He had a hold of me physically, mentally, and emotionally.

He would cry, beg, and promise a thousand times that he wasn't doing things I knew he was doing.

He'd change for a few days, but he always went back to his old ways.

I had a prayer life. I prayed, but I didn't believe any of the things I said. God knew I was insincere.

Oh, but when you have people praying for you, interceding on your behalf, and covering you, God will work behind the scenes to answer their prayers.

He knows what is best for you!

After multiple abortions, having a baby to term was a source of worry for me. I feared that God wouldn't allow it since I'd killed my other babies.

However, God is not a vengeful God. My pregnancy went smoothly and although my relationship was toxic, my baby was a blessing.

In 2012, I became a mother. Giving birth to my sweet baby girl was the beginning of positive change in my life.

I stayed with my daughter's father after she was born, but something new began to take root in me.

I no longer felt that I needed him to complete me. The desire to deal with the things he was doing began to leave me.

I had a baby that needed me. Having this child made the way clear for me to leave because I didn't want her to grow up to be like me. I didn't want her to believe that she was worthless or that she didn't deserve love.

I wanted to teach her self-worth, love, and the concept of having healthy boundaries. I wanted my baby to know that respect should be given and earned.

After many years of wrong thinking, God began to renew my mind, and I began to think clearly. I knew what I needed to do.

Thank You, God!

S.H.E made it, and S.H.E is the JOY of my life!

Another thing I want you to know is that you must be careful what you speak.

"Death and life are in the power of the tongue; and they that love it shall eat the fruit thereof." (Proverbs 18:21)

During my time of confusion, God still blessed me with the desires of my heart.

I wanted love that would never change, that I could give my all to, and that would be there forever. He gave me that in my sweet, baby girl.

One thing about God is this; He will give you everything you ask for in order to show you that it's not good for you.

I had to learn to trust that God knows what is best for me. Even when I don't understand what is going on, I have to trust the process.

"She opens her mouth with wisdom and in her tongue is the law of kindness."

(Proverbs 31:26)

"Leaving Hurt and Getting Healed."
Sparkling Bwtee

"And my God will meet all your needs according to the riches of his glory in Christ Jesus."
(Philippians 4:19)

Something Beautiful
A Song by Tori Kelly

Breathe in and let it go,

Oh, your tears are not for nothing

Let them fall off

In every teardrop there is something beautiful,

Oh, you are stronger than you know,

Oh,

Oh, you're something beautiful!

S.H.E.

Who is S.H.E?
Is S.H.E me?
How can S.H.E be me?
S.H.E knows that God is the head of her life!
S.H.E knows that she is resilient.
S.H.E loves herself enough **NOT** to settle.
S.H.E is confident in whom God created her to be.
S.H.E is the one who is better than before.
S.H.E is the one healed & delivered from past mistakes.
S.H.E is empowering other women with her story.
S.H.E is the one who knows where she's headed.
S.H.E is the one who's different than the rest.
S.H.E is a fighter who **NEVER** gives up!
S.H.E is the one who is worthy and deserving!
S.H.E is **NEVER** intimidated.
S.H.E is courageous!
S.H.E is the one who sets goals for her future.
S.H.E is the prize!
S.H.E knows that there is *MORE* to life than what's she
been used to!
S.H.E is my hero!
So, who is S.H.E?
S.H.E is You and S.H.E is Me too!

Go out and sparkle with a purpose!

Sparkling Bwtee

About the Author

Author Tiffina Williams sets the tone for her day by beginning with prayer. Through her ministry, "Sparkling Bwtee2, LLC," Tiffina strives to uplift, encourage, motivate, and inspire women all over the world. She wants women to know that they are beautiful, just the way God created them.

"Look at life with a different perspective," Tiffina proclaims. "I never want a person to leave me the same as when they met me!"

With a bright smile, wisdom, and love of people, Tiffina leaves a lasting impression on the hearts and minds of those with whom she connects.

"When times get tough," the author declares, "trusting God is what I stand on to make it through."

Having MC or spoken at various women's events, Tiffina's lifestyle journey is all about empowering women to embrace their differences as well as their challenges. She wants women to understand that no matter what has happened in their lives, God can change your life around. He will use your story for His glory!

Tiffina Una Williams currently resides in Missouri where she is a prayer warrior, servant, daughter, mother, sister, motivator, leader, and friend to many.

Whether by T-shirts sales, social media posts (Video blogs, Facebook, Instagram, and Blog posts), Williams reminds every woman to, "*Go Out and Sparkle With A Purpose.*"

To reach Williams for speaking engagements, email her at sparklingbwtee@yahoo.com.

"We Believe in Your Dreams"

Iris M. Williams

Butterfly Typeface Publishing

PO Box 56193

Little Rock AR 72215

info@butterflytypeface.com

www.ingramcontent.com/pod-product-compliance
Lightning Source LLC
Chambersburg PA
CBHW051733020426
42333CB00014B/1288